Y0-ABY-178

Animal Wisecrackers

H. AARON COHL

Animal Wisecrackers
Copyright © 2006, Silverback Books, Inc.

All rights reserved. No part of this book may be
used or reproduced in any manner whatsoever
without prior written permission of the publisher.

Photographs courtesy of Jupiterimages.
Used with permission. All rights reserved.

Cover design by Richard Garnas
Interior design and production by Patty Holden

ISBN: 1-59637-064-5

Printed and bound in China

Introduction

We know they are thinking about something. That sinister shifting of their eyes is a dead giveaway. Or, maybe it's a subtle change in posture, or a feigned "smile." Whatever the case may be, we know they are planning, conniving, and conspiring. But to what end? We can sense their feeling of physical superiority, their sheer bravado in being able to weather the elements without clothes, their jealousy in not being able to cook a hot meal, and their disdain for our opposable thumbs (except for our simian cousins, of course, who have other issues with us). From playful to mischievous, sarcastic to sardonic, the animal kingdom has been mocking and challenging us behind our backs from time immemorial. No longer. Finally, the "animal code" has been cracked!

Yeah, I'll share.
When pigs fly.

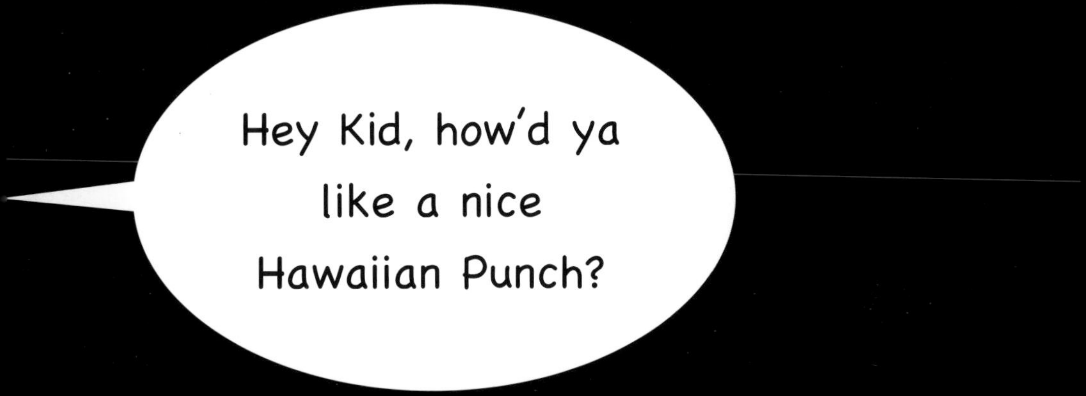
Hey Kid, how'd ya like a nice Hawaiian Punch?

Hmmm. I wonder if I should try the Atkins diet?

Come on!
Cookies and...water!?
What planet are
you from?

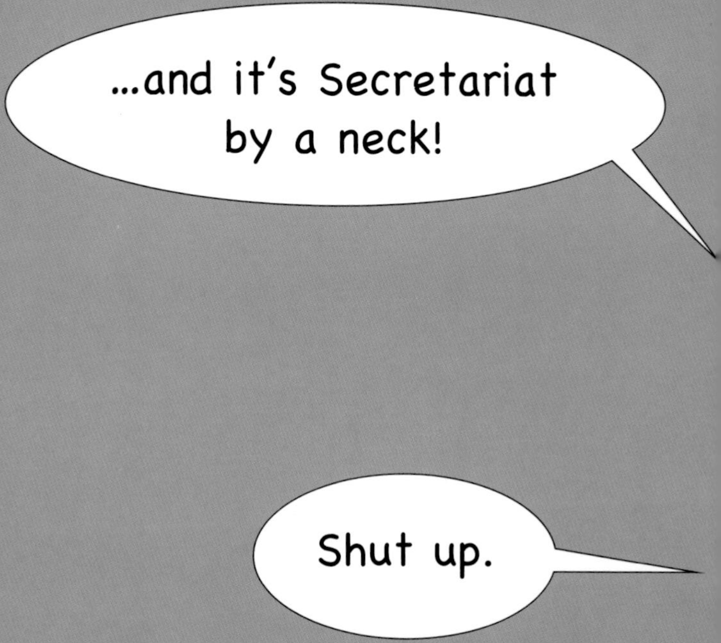
...and it's Secretariat by a neck!
Shut up.

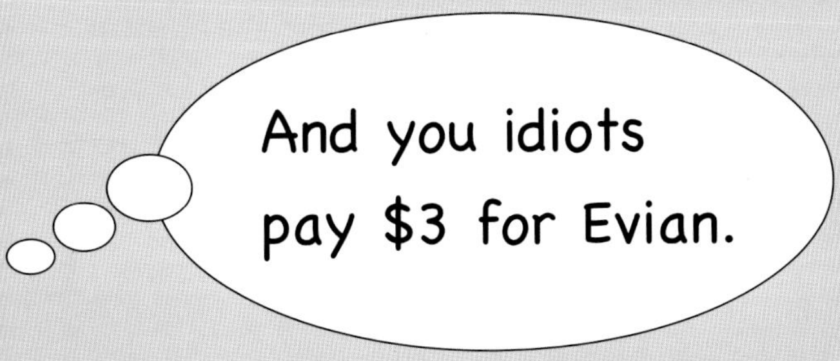
And you idiots pay $3 for Evian.

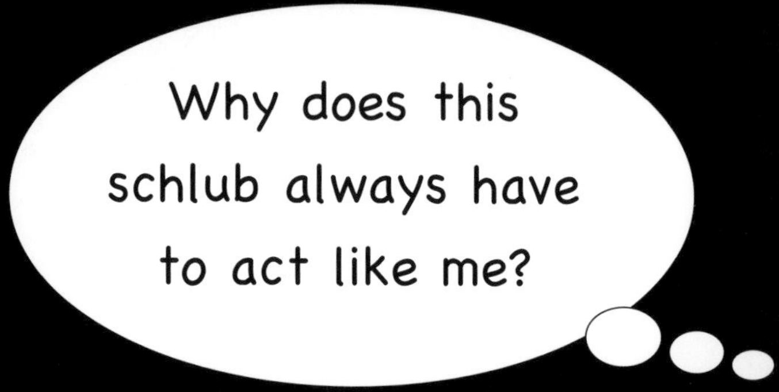
Why does this schlub always have to act like me?

Throw the ball now, you little brat, or I'll chew your arm off.

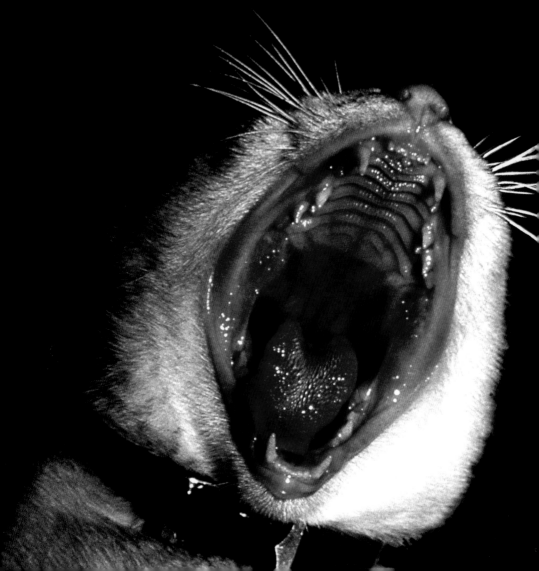

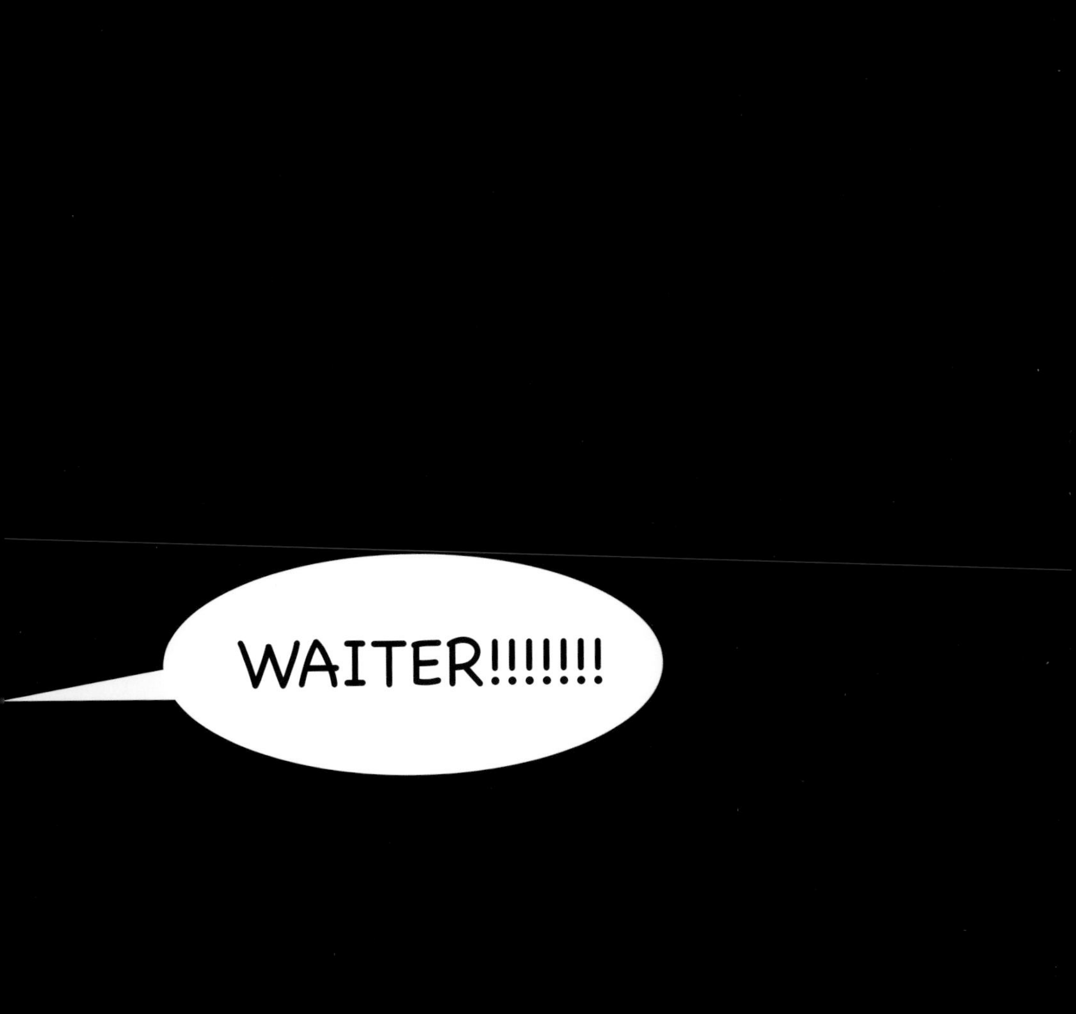
WAITER!!!!!!!

What do you say, Big X,
three tunnels? Tom, Dick,
and Harry?

Son, you're
watching wayyyy
too much TV.

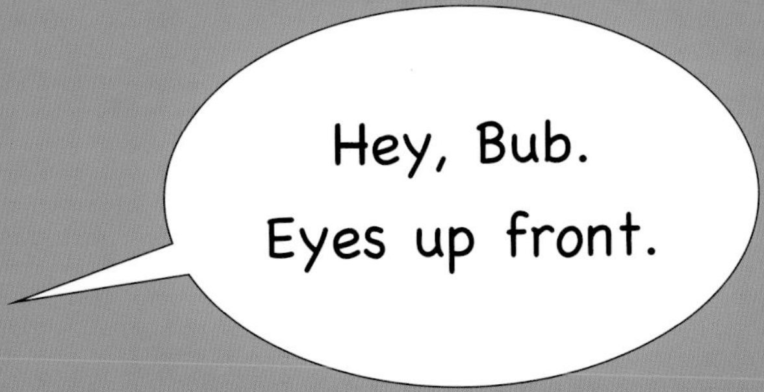
Hey, Bub.
Eyes up front.

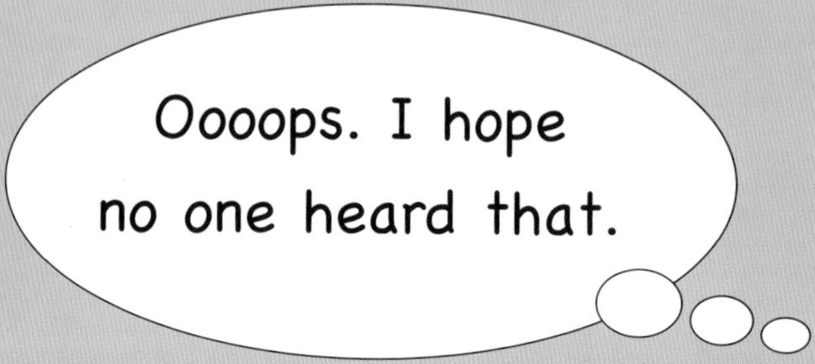
Oooops. I hope no one heard that.

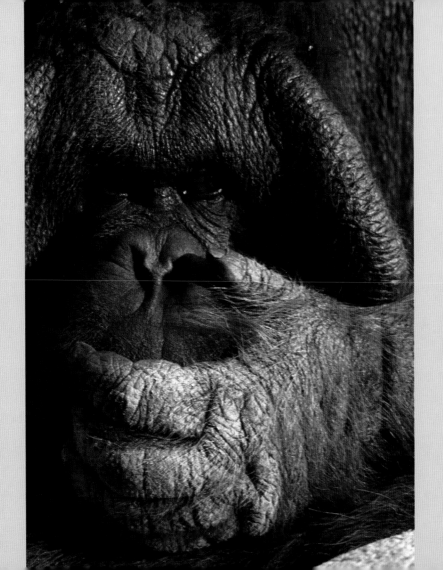

Ahhhhh.
Sushi.

Don't be such a chicken. Just ask the dame for more grub.

Yeow!
Those peppers
are HOT!!!

I know it's not
a real mouse!

So this is what it's like to be Martha Stewart.

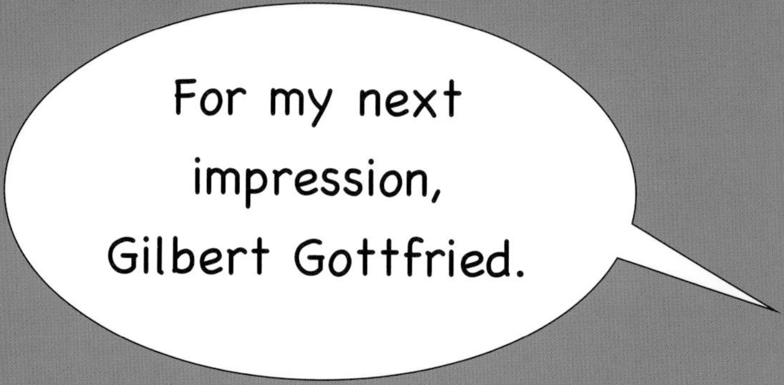
For my next impression, Gilbert Gottfried.

That's what
I'm talking about!
Screw the puppy chow.

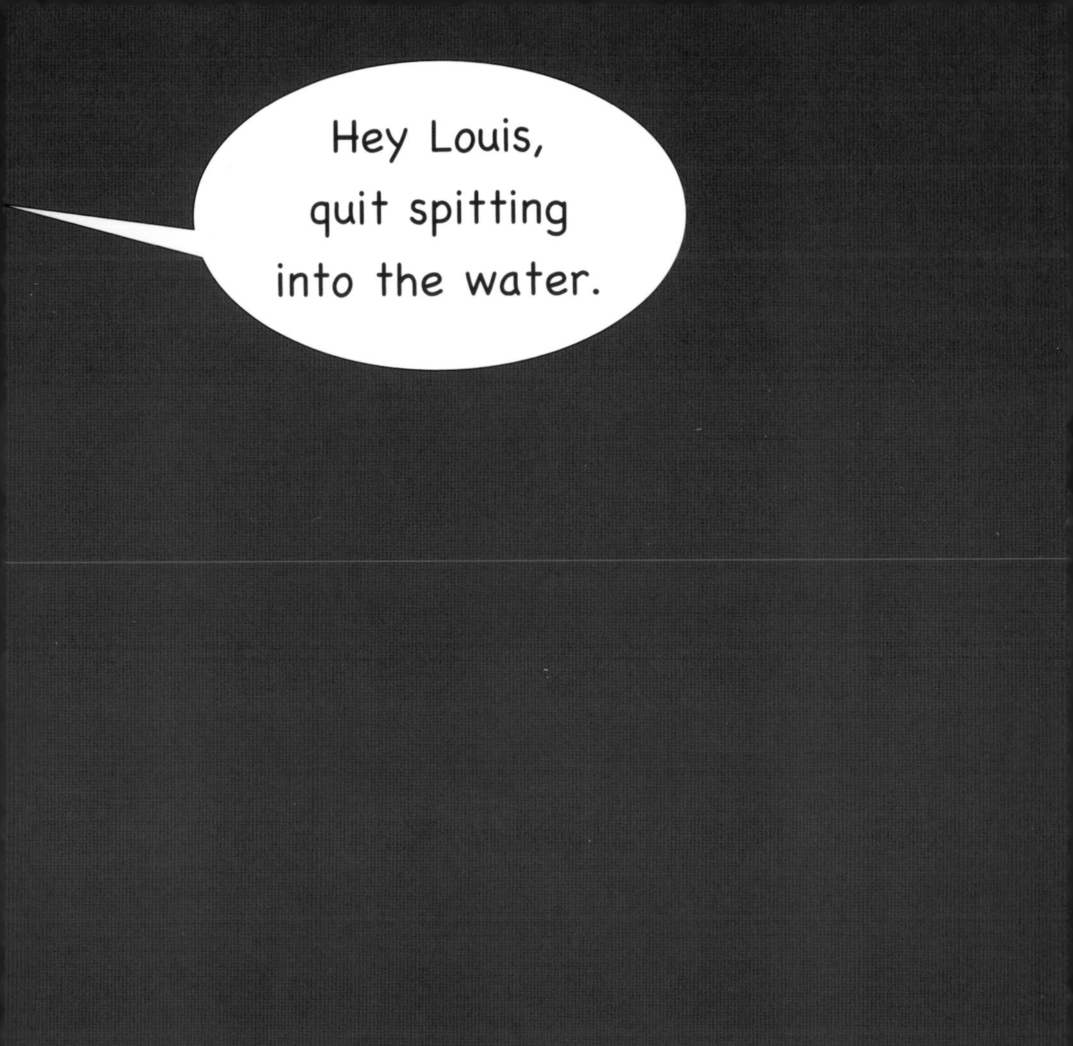
Hey Louis, quit spitting into the water.

God, how I love peanut butter.

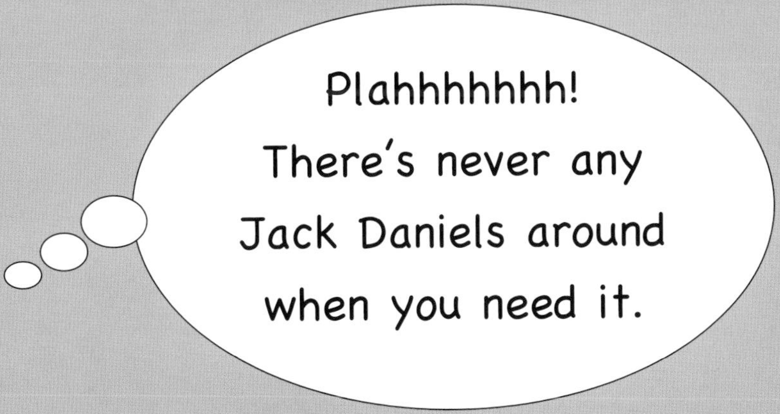
Plahhhhhhh!
There's never any
Jack Daniels around
when you need it.

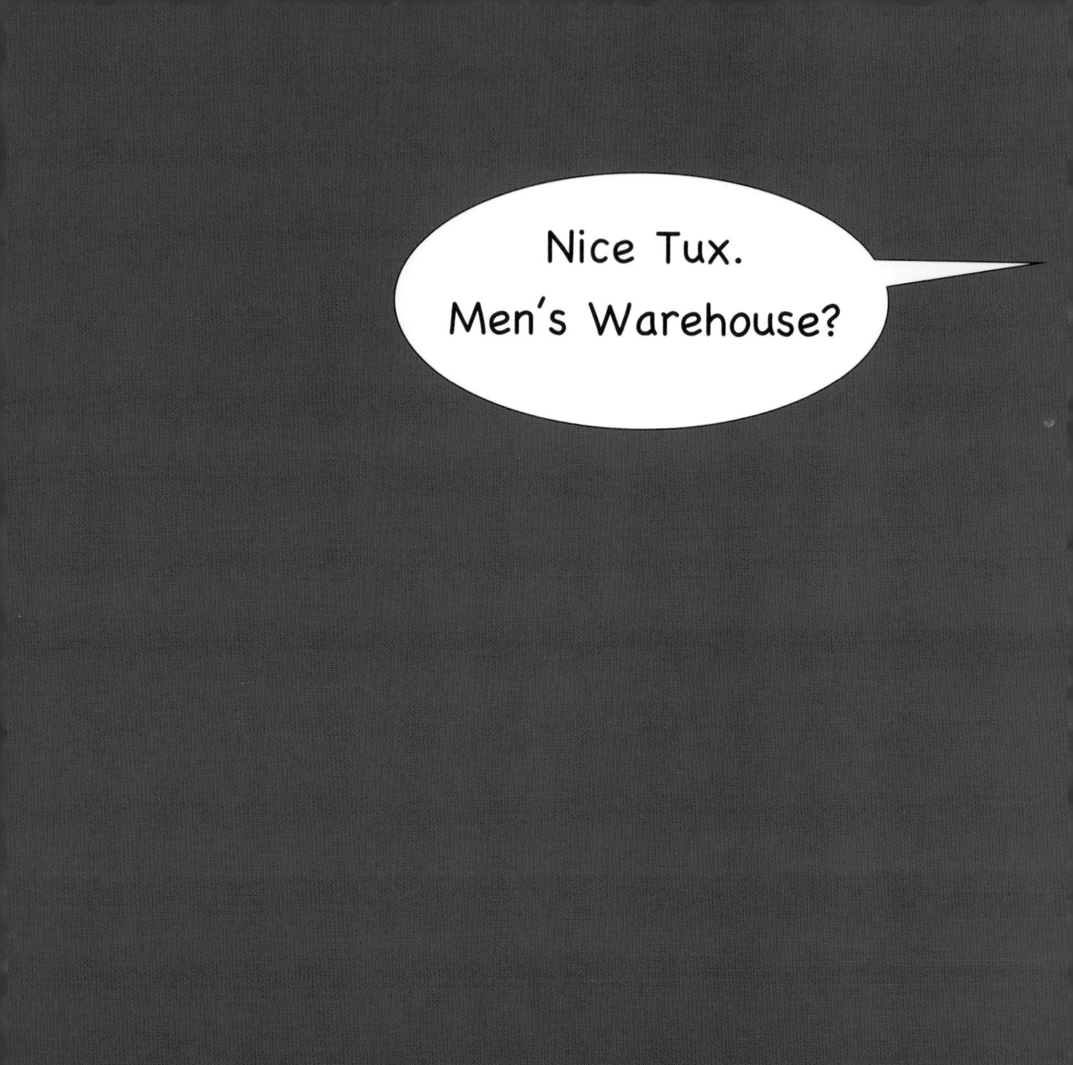
Nice Tux. Men's Warehouse?

If I'm your best friend,
how come you don't
feed me steak?

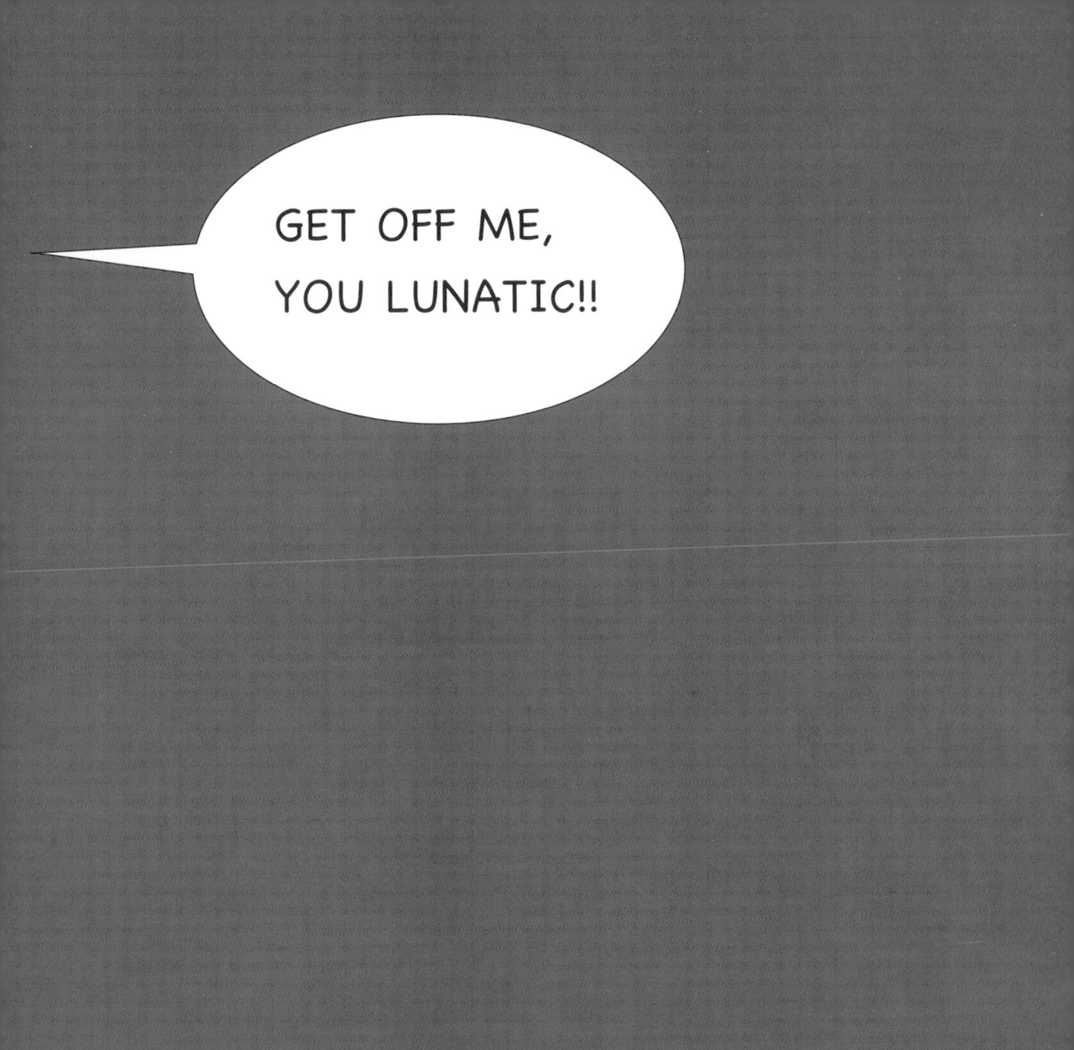
GET OFF ME, YOU LUNATIC!!

Excuse me, Ma'am,
but could you spare
a ham sandwich?

We'd make
much better pilots
than you people.

Heavens to Betsy!
How long does it take
to open a can of
dog food?

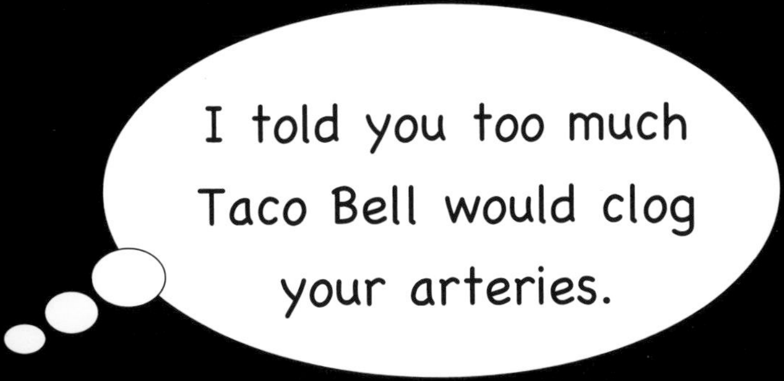
I told you too much Taco Bell would clog your arteries.

There's not a
prison on this planet
that can hold me, the
Great Houndini.

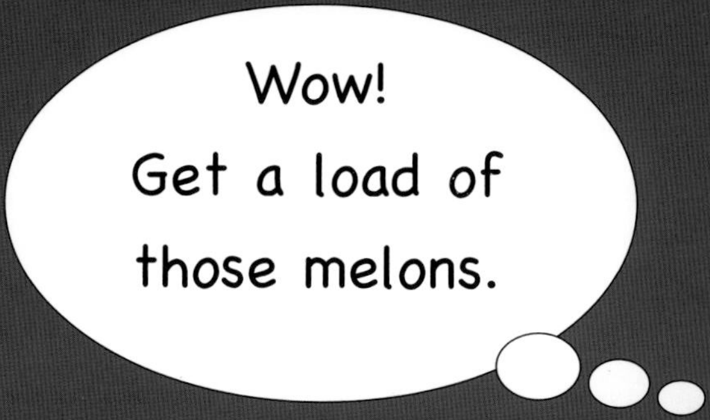
Wow!
Get a load of
those melons.

Herb, if you had
an ounce of moxie,
I'd be the Aflac
duck and we'd be
retired by now.

Just one more lick. No one will ever notice.

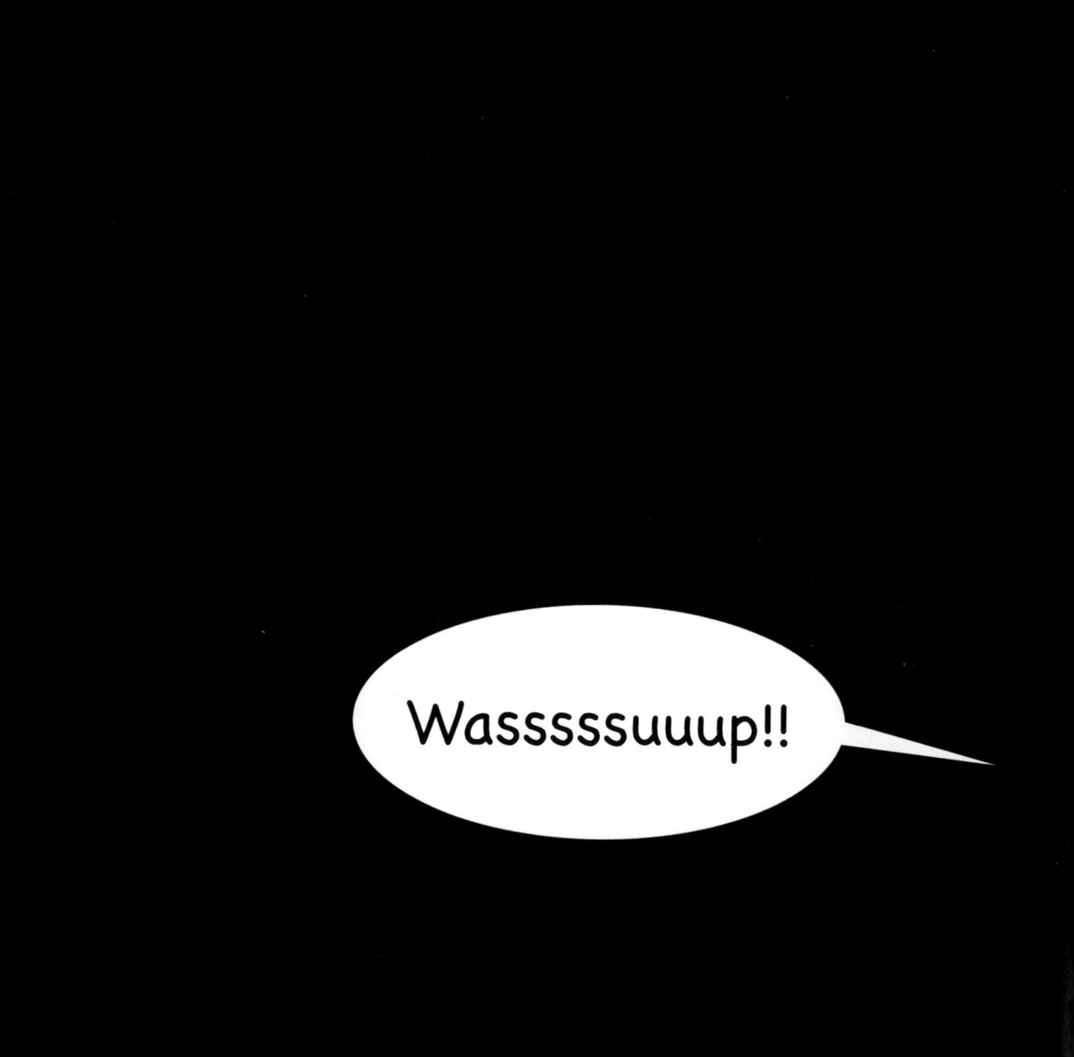
Wasssssuuup!!

You two sit this one out. Let the master show you how to deal with the paparazzi.

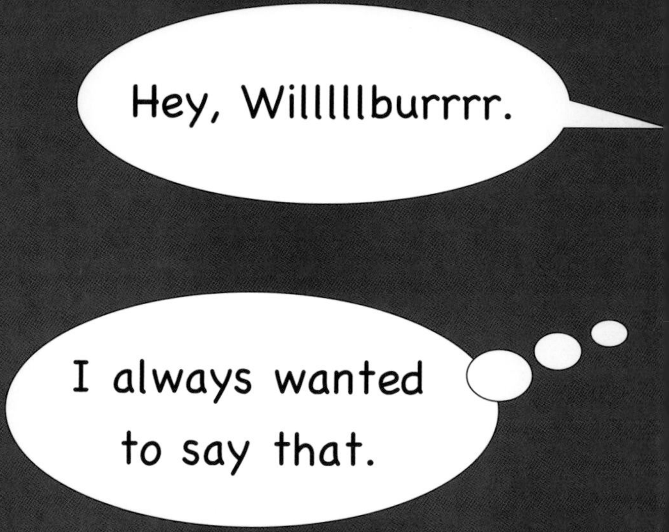
Hey, Willlllburrrr.
I always wanted to say that.

PHOTO CREDITS

COVER PHOTO: Ibid; P. 4: Alley Cat Productions; P. 7: Alley Cat Productions; P. 8: Echos; P. 11: Photo 24; P. 12: Michael Donnelly; P. 15: Photo 24; P. 16: Andersen Ross; P. 19: Untitled; P. 20: SW Productions; P. 23: Alley Cat Productions; P. 24: David Troncoso; P. 27: Alexandra Grablewski; P. 28: es; P. 31: Photo 24; P. 32: Alley Cat Productions; P. 35: Alley Cat Productions; P. 36: Ray Kachatorian; P. 39: Alley Cat Productions; P. 40: Ibid; P. 43: Alley Cat Productions; P. 44: Tim Hawley; P. 47: Ibid; P. 48: TongRo Image Stock; P. 51: Ibid; P. 52: Alley Cat Productions; P. 55: Ralph Steckler; P. 56: Ibid; P. 59: Untitled; P. 60: Echos; P. 63: pbnj productions; P. 64: Echos; P. 67: Don Mason; P. 68: Steven Puetzer; P. 71: Ibid; P. 72: Bill Boch; P. 75: Alley Cat Productions; P. 76: Ibid; P. 79: Ibid; P. 80: Melanie Acevedo; P. 83: Andreas Bleckmann; P. 84: Ibid; P. 87: Ibid.

The beautiful photos you see throughout this book are courtesy of Jupiterimages.
For more information on the contributing photographers, visit www.jupiterimages.com.

jupiterimages.